T0417729

URSA

MARVELS OF TECHNOLOGY

VEHICLE & TRANSPORT TECH

by
Anita Loughrey and Alex Woolf

BEARPORT
PUBLISHING

Minneapolis, Minnesota

Credits

Cover and title page, © Leonid Andronov/Shutterstock and © Alassar/Shutterstock 4, © Attapon Thana/Shutterstock; 4–5, © NH/Shutterstock; 5, © aapsky/iStock; 6TR, © steamroller_blues/Shutterstock; 6M, © Pichi/Shutterstock; 6BL, © Birmingham Museums Trust/Wikimedia commons; 6–7, © Pablo Vasco/Shutterstock; 7T, © cristi180884/ Shutterstock; 8ML, © Milatoo/iStock; 8BL, © Jim West/Alamy; 8–9, © sylv1rob1/Shutterstock; 9BL, © Public domain/ US Patent and Trademark Office; 10MR, © VECTORWORKS_ENTERPRISE/Shutterstock; 10BL, © Shutterstock; 10–11, © Steve Bower/Shutterstock; 11TL, © Hein Nouwens/Shutterstock; 12ML, © VectorMine/Shutterstock; 12BR, © kynny/ iStock; 12–13, © piranka/iStock; 14MR, © KsanderDN/Shutterstock; 14BL, © Martin Sanders/Beehive Illustration; 14–15, © Benoist/Shutterstock; 15BL, © Petr Born/Shutterstock; 16M, © Martin Sanders/Beehive Illustration; 16BL, © Public domain/Wikimedia commons; 16–17, © alice-photo/Shutterstock; 17MR, © Pavel L Photo and Video/ Shutterstock; 18ML, © Mongta Studio/Shutterstock; 18MR, © Sergey Bogdanov/Shutterstock; 18BL, © CAEV.weebly. com/Wikimedia commons 18–19, © aappp/Shutterstock; 19TR, © Zapylaiev Kostiantyn/Shutterstock; 20ML, © Chesky/ Shutterstock; 20–21, © Skycolors/Shutterstock; 21BL, © Imperial War Museums/Wikimedia commons; 22M, © Martin Sanders/Beehive Illustration; 22BL, © Dibner Library of the History of Science and Technology/Wikimedia commons; 22–23, © freevideophotoagency/Shutterstock; 23TR, © Martin Sanders/Beehive Illustration; 23BL, © Sergiy1975/ Shutterstock; 24ML, © Sergey Merkulov/Shutterstock; 24–25, © FotograFFF/Shutterstock; 25TL, © Granger Historical Picture Archive/ Alamy; 26ML, © dani3315/Shutterstock; 26B, © Martin Sanders/Beehive Illustration; 26–27, © Andrea Danti/Shutterstock; 27T, © Andrea Danti/Shutterstock; 27BL, © Public domain/Wikimedia commons; 28ML, © SimpleB/ Shutterstock; 28–29, © Dmitry Kalinovsky/Shutterstock; 29BL, © Smithsonian Institution/Wikimedia commons; 30ML, © SHINPANU/Shutterstock; 30BL, © andrey_l/Shutterstock; 30–31, © Suwin66/Shutterstock; 31BL, © BasPhoto/ Shutterstock; 32–33, © 3Dsculptor/Shutterstock; 33T, © Kim Shiflett/NASA; 33BR, © NASA; 33BL, © Goddard/NASA; 34ML, © Stockbyte/Getty; 34BL, © Triff/Shutterstock; 34–35, © Juergen Faelchle/Shutterstock; 35, © Devrimb/iStock; 35BL, © hkipix/Alamy; 36ML, © Wang An Qi/Shutterstock; 36BR, © Crown/Met Office; 36–37, © aappp/Shutterstock; 37TR, © EUMETSAT; 37BL, © ITU Pictures/Wikimedia commons; 38MR, © Martin Sanders /Beehive Illustration; 38BL, © US Navy; 38–39, © Pincasso/Shutterstock and © Yuri Bizgaimer/Adobe Stock; 39TL, © Yulai Studio/Shutterstock; 40ML, © Martin Sanders/Beehive Illustration; 40BL, © Liebherr-International Deutschland GmbH (Biberach an der Riß); 40–41, © gd_project/Shutterstock; 41TR, © astudio/Shutterstock; 42BL, © metamorworks/iStock; 42–43, © kolesinibimitresku/Shutterstock; 43MR, © andrey_l/Shutterstock; 44, © aappp/Shutterstock; 45TL, © SimpleB/ Shutterstock; 45BL, © Triff/Shutterstock; 47, © Steve Bower/Shutterstock

Bearport Publishing Company Product Development Team
President: Jen Jenson; Director of Product Development: Spencer Brinker; Managing Editor: Allison Juda; Associate Editor: Naomi Reich; Associate Editor: Tiana Tran; Art Director: Colin O'Dea; Designer: Kim Jones; Designer: Kayla Eggert; Product Development Assistant: Owen Hamlin

Statement on Usage of Generative Artificial Intelligence
Bearport Publishing remains committed to publishing high-quality nonfiction books. Therefore, we restrict the use of generative AI to ensure accuracy of all text and visual components pertaining to a book's subject. See BearportPublishing.com for details.

Library of Congress Cataloging-in-Publication Data is available at www.loc.gov or upon request from the publisher.

ISBN: 979-8-89232-086-3 (hardcover)
ISBN: 979-8-89232-618-6 (paperback)
ISBN: 979-8-89232-219-5 (ebook)

For more information, write to Bearport Publishing, 5357 Penn Avenue South, Minneapolis, MN 55419.

Contents

Vehicle Tech

At its most basic, technology is simple. It's the application of scientific knowledge to create products that solve problems and make our lives easier. But what technology can do is pretty amazing.

Meeting Our Needs

New technologies are developed to meet our ever-evolving needs. For example, seat belts alone are not always an effective enough defense against high speed vehicle collisions. Inflatable air bags were developed to be used along with seat belts for extra protection. They deploy instantly during a crash and cushion the passengers' upper bodies and heads from potentially harmful impacts.

Most airbags can deploy in only 20 to 30 milliseconds. That's faster than the blink of an eye!

Solving Problems

Technology can change as our needs change. We want to get places fast. Passenger trains can travel more than 100 miles per hour (160 kph). But speed is not always safe. Trains have derailed going too fast around tight curves. So, engineers have developed new onboard computer systems that monitor speed for both efficiency and safety. These systems can automatically turn on the brakes if trains are moving too fast.

The advancement of technology allows engineers and designers to create vehicles that have never been seen before.

Designing Tomorrow's Vehicles

Every day, designers are working to innovate the performance of cars, buses, trucks, trains, ships, planes, and spacecraft. They are trying to improve the way our current vehicles function and solve the problems they have. Designers are working hard to develop vehicles that not only function well and are reliable, but also are comfortable, safe, and stylish.

Bicycles

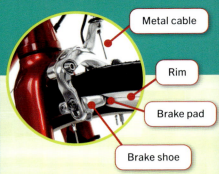

Metal cable

Rim

Brake pad

Brake shoe

A bicycle uses pedals to drive a chain, which moves wheels and propels the bike forward. Gears change the distance the bicycle moves with each pedal stroke. They enable the rider to maintain a comfortable pedaling speed, whether cycling uphill, downhill, or on a level surface.

Brakes

Thin metal cables run from the brake levers on the handlebars to the front and back wheels. When the rider squeezes the levers, the cables pull on the brake shoes, forcing the brake pads to press against the rims of the wheels. This friction slows the bicycle down.

Gears

Gears are a set of toothed wheels that hold the bike's chain. They are attached to the axle of the bike's rear wheel. The largest gear is farthest from the frame and needs the least pedaling force to turn. This is often used when riding uphill. The smallest gear needs the most pedaling force to turn it, but it allows the bicycle to travel farther with each rotation. It is useful for riders going downhill.

When a rider changes gear, the chain moves to the selected gear.

INVENTION

Inventor: John Kemp Starley

Invention: Rover Safety Bicycle

Date: 1885

The story: British inventor John Kemp Starley developed the modern design for a bicycle. It had equal-sized wheels, a chain to turn the rear wheel, and a steerable front wheel. His bicycle was more stable than previous designs.

DID YOU KNOW? Olympic bicycles have wheels without spokes, which allows for improved airflow, reduced drag, and faster speeds.

The gear shifters are the controls that change the gears. They are attached to the derailleurs by gear cables.

Brake lever

Most bicycles have a diamond frame created with two triangles of hollow tube. The strong triangle shape positions the rider's weight between the back and front wheels.

Handlebars

Frame

Saddle

The back derailleur changes the gear by moving the bottom of the chain from side to side. It contains a spring to keep a constant tension on the chain.

Pedal

Gears

The front derailleur shifts the chain between the front gears.

Chain

Wheel

Electric Bikes

Riding a bike can be a lot of fun . . . until you come across a steep hill. But in recent years, electric bikes, or e-bikes, have made going uphill a breeze. These bikes have electric motors that boost propulsion, reaching speeds of almost 30 mph (48 kph)—with very little effort from the rider.

There are two kinds of e-bikes: pedal-assist and power-on-demand. With pedal-assist, the electric motor helps move the bike forward only while the rider is pedaling. Meanwhile, the motor on a power-on-demand bike is activated by a handlebar throttle similar to one found on a moped. The throttle powers the bike forward even when the rider is not pedaling. Some e-bikes have both pedal-assist and power-on-demand throttles.

Electric Bike

E-bike motors are powered by rechargeable batteries. Most are charged by being plugged into an outlet, but some get small amounts of energy every time the rider uses the brakes. Depending on the type of bike, terrain, speed, and battery size, most e-bikes can travel 20–30 miles (32–48 km) on a single charge. Some bigger batteries can power an e-bike for 100 miles (160 km).

DID YOU KNOW? Karl Drais invented the first bicycle in 1817. It had no pedals. A rider moved forward by pushing off the ground with their feet.

Throttle

Some e-bikes have a front basket that can hold small bags or other items as the rider bikes.

Inventor: Ogden Bolton Jr.

Invention: Battery-powered bicycle

Date: 1895

The story: Ogden Bolton Jr. installed a motor on the rear wheel hub of a bike. The motor was powered by a 10-volt battery. This design earned him the very first patent for a battery-powered bicycle.

INVENTION

Cars

Most cars are powered by an internal combustion engine that produces energy by burning a mixture of compressed fuel and air. Sparks ignite the air-fuel mix, pushing a set of pistons. These pistons rotate the crankshaft, which turns the driveshaft. The driveshaft is connected to the car's axle, causing the wheels to turn and moving the car forward.

Four-stroke Sequence

Inside the engine is a row of metal cylinders containing pistons. The pistons move in a four-stroke sequence.

1 When the piston moves down, it drags fuel and air into the cylinder through an inlet valve.

2 When the inlet valve closes, the piston moves up inside the cylinder, compressing the fuel and air mixture. A spark in the spark plug ignites the mixture, producing hot gases.

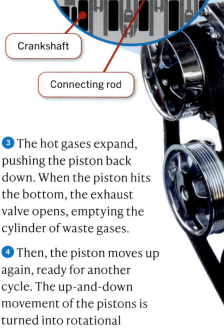

Spark plug • Piston • Cylinder • Crankshaft • Connecting rod

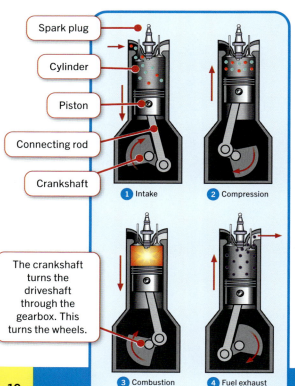

Spark plug

Cylinder

Piston

Connecting rod

Crankshaft

1 Intake

2 Compression

The crankshaft turns the driveshaft through the gearbox. This turns the wheels.

3 Combustion

4 Fuel exhaust

3 The hot gases expand, pushing the piston back down. When the piston hits the bottom, the exhaust valve opens, emptying the cylinder of waste gases.

4 Then, the piston moves up again, ready for another cycle. The up-and-down movement of the pistons is turned into rotational movement by the crankshaft.

10

Inventor: Margaret A. Wilcox

Invention: Car heater

Date: 1893

The story: American mechanical engineer Margaret A. Wilcox developed a way to direct air from the engine inside the car to produce heat. Her invention is the basis of car heaters today.

The engine sucks in air and fuel.

A battery provides electricity for the spark to ignite the air and fuel mixture.

Oil allows the metal parts to move easily.

Water pumped from the radiator keeps the engine cool.

Electric and Hybrid Cars

For a hundred years after Carl Benz invented the first modern car in 1885, car engines were powered by gasoline. But since the 1990s, engineers have been inventing cars that run partly or fully on battery-powered electricity.

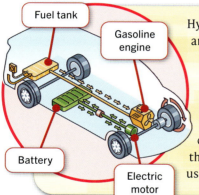

Fuel tank

Gasoline engine

Battery

Electric motor

Hybrid cars are powered by a gasoline engine, an electric motor, and a battery. The battery-powered electric motor is used when the car is traveling at low speeds, and the gas engine takes over at higher speeds, during acceleration, or when the car is climbing a hill. The car's brakes capture the friction energy generated when the car coasts or slows down. The car then uses this energy to recharge the battery.

A fully electric car is powered by only a battery. It has no engine and uses no fuel. The battery provides an electric current to the motor, which propels the car's wheels. To recharge the battery, users plug the car into a charging station. Most electric cars can travel about 300 miles (480 km) before having to be recharged.

DID YOU KNOW? The first full-scale, self-propelled mechanical vehicle was invented in 1769 by Nicolas-Joseph Cugnot. It was a steam-powered tricycle!

Different kinds of charging stations power cars at different speeds.

CHARGING 74%

INVENTION

Inventor: Robert Anderson

Invention: An electric carriage

Date: 1832–1839

The story: Robert Anderson strapped a battery and motor onto his carriage rather than using horses for power. The battery did not push the horseless carriage very far or very fast, but it was a major step forward in battery-powered vehicles.

Car Safety

Some car safety features are designed to avoid collisions. These include mirrors, lights, horns, and anti-lock braking systems, which prevent wheels from locking and the car skidding during heavy braking. Other safety features are designed to protect the driver and passengers in the event of a collision. These include seat belts and airbags.

A wheel speed sensor determines if the wheel is trying to lock up during braking.

If the wheel tries to lock up, hydraulic valves limit braking to prevent the vehicle from skidding.

Airbags

Airbags are made from nylon. They are fitted into the steering wheel, dashboard, and doors of vehicles. Airbags have three parts: the bag itself, a sensor, and an inflation system. The sensor contains an accelerometer, which is a device used for measuring the acceleration of a moving body. If the sensor detects a collision, it sends an electric current through a heating element in the inflation system. The heat causes two chemicals, sodium azide and potassium nitrate, to react and produce a blast of nitrogen gas that inflates the airbag.

An airbag inflates in 0.03 seconds.

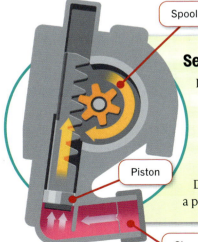

Spool

Piston

Chamber of explosive gas

Seat Belts

Inside the seat belt casing is a retractor mechanism. It consists of a spool and a spring. When the belt is pulled, the spool rotates and the spring untwists. When the belt is let go, the spring twists back, rotating the spool, and tightening the belt. The seat belt also has a mechanism called a pre-tensioner with a chamber of explosive gas. During a crash, an electric current ignites the gas, pushing a piston that rotates the spool, tightening the belt.

DID YOU KNOW? The first cars had no steering wheel. People steered them with a lever.

Crash dummies are used to test seat belts and airbags. The dummies are built to react in a similar way to the human body.

A car seat belt locks when given a sharp tug. During a car crash, this keeps the driver and passengers in their seats.

Inventor: Mary Anderson

Invention: Windshield wiper

Date: 1903

The story: American inventor Mary Anderson was visiting New York and noticed streetcar drivers wiping snow off their windshields by hand. This prompted her to design a rubber blade that could be fitted outside the windshield and controlled by a lever inside the vehicle.

INVENTION

Traffic Lights

Traffic lights determine a person's right-of-way at road intersections. Some traffic lights are set with timers. These lights change after a predetermined length of time. Most, however, are controlled by sensors. These count the number of cars approaching the intersection from each direction and keep the busier routes green for a longer time.

Sensors

Sensor-controlled traffic lights use sensors called induction loops—magnets with loops of wire—embedded in the road surface. When a car drives over the sensor, it changes the magnetic field. An electrical signal is sent to a computer controlling the traffic light. Each sequence of red-yellow-green lights is called a phase. The computer is programmed to let a certain time elapse before a new phase can begin.

A computer controls the traffic light.

The inductance meter measures the strength of the signal.

When a vehicle is detected, the induction loop sends a signal to the inductance meter.

Induction loops are buried beneath the road's surface.

INVENTOR

Inventor: Garrett Morgan

Invention: Three-position traffic lights

Date: 1923

The story: American inventor Garrett Morgan made the first traffic lights with three colors, adding the yellow light. At night, the lights could be set so the yellow light blinked to warn drivers to use caution at intersections.

Detection camera

Red

Yellow

Green

Traffic Control

Cameras are often placed on fast roads, busy intersections, bridges, and tunnels. The video information is transmitted to a traffic management room, where traffic lights can be controlled to help move the traffic efficiently. This helps prevent congestion and accidents.

Traffic management rooms have large screens. This provides the people controlling traffic with real-time images of busy intersections 24 hours a day.

Traffic lights enable road users to pass safely through intersections and help regulate traffic during busy times of the day.

DID YOU KNOW? A red light has a longer wavelength than green, so it can be seen from farther away. This gives drivers a longer time to brake.

Trains

Diesel trains contain powerful two-stroke diesel engines. Unlike four-stroke car engines, the pistons in diesel engines complete a two-stroke cycle. The fuel is injected directly into the compressed air. Electric trains often get their electricity from a third rail running alongside the track, which drives motors on their wheels.

Points

Points are the switches that enable trains to change tracks. Part of the track, called the blade, moves and guides the wheels at the junction where the tracks meet.

Blade

Flange

Train tracks are bolted to sleepers. These spacers beneath the tracks keep the tracks the correct distance apart.

Rail

Inventor: Robert Davidson

Invention: Electric train

Date: 1837

The story: Scottish chemist Robert Davidson designed and made the first electric train. It had four wheels and was powered by batteries. In 1842, he tested the train on the Edinburgh-Glasgow railway line.

INVENTOR

Some trains get their electricity from overhead cables.

Signals

Signals tell the train driver when to stop and when it is safe to move. Today, they are controlled automatically by computers in a control room. Before this, signals were operated by hand using levers. A lever would change the signal and move the points on a track.

Trains have metal wheels with a rim on the inside called a flange. Flanges stop the wheels from slipping off the tracks.

DID YOU KNOW? The world's longest train journey is between Moscow, Russia, and Pyongyang, North Korea. It takes almost eight days.

Planes

A plane creates lift with its wings and is thrust forward by its engines. A jet engine works on the same principle as a car engine: it burns fuel and air to release energy. But instead of using cylinders and pistons, a jet engine consists of one long metal tube. Air is drawn in at the front end of the tube and is compressed by a fan. Then, the air is mixed with fuel and combusted. Finally, it is blasted out the back of the tube as hot exhaust, creating thrust.

Turbo Jet Engine

A fan at the front of the jet engine sucks in cold air. Then, a second fan called a compressor squeezes the air, increasing its temperature and pressure. Kerosene fuel is squirted into the engine, where it gets mixed with the compressed air and combusts.

Nose

Turbine

Hot waste gases exit the engine through an exhaust nozzle. The narrow nozzle helps accelerate the gases, so they are moving at twice the speed of the cold air entering at the front.

Exhaust

Ailerons help the plane stay level. To change direction, the ailerons are raised on one wing and lowered on the other.

Combustor

Fuel and air mix and ignite in the combustion chamber.

Shaft

Fan

Compressor

Air is squeezed as it travels through compressors.

DID YOU KNOW? During World War II (1939–1945), the United States made a huge, eight-engine flying boat. It was nicknamed the *Spruce Goose*.

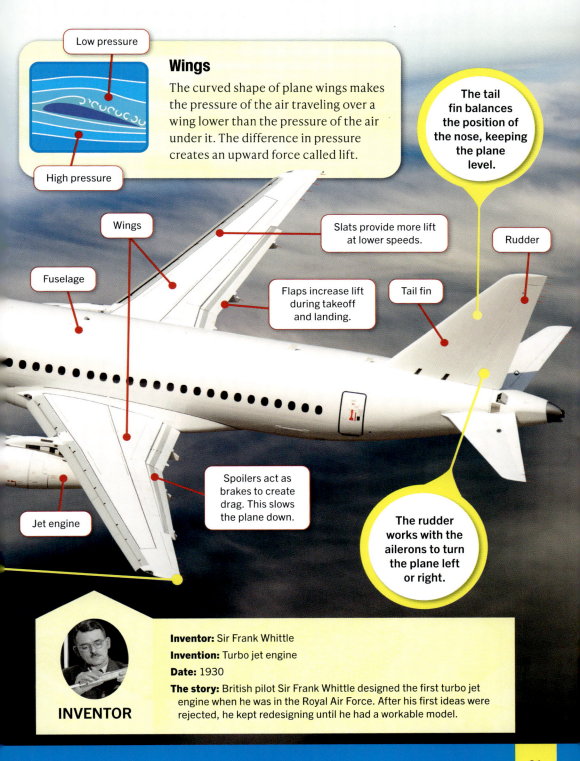

Low pressure

Wings

The curved shape of plane wings makes the pressure of the air traveling over a wing lower than the pressure of the air under it. The difference in pressure creates an upward force called lift.

High pressure

The tail fin balances the position of the nose, keeping the plane level.

Wings

Slats provide more lift at lower speeds.

Rudder

Fuselage

Flaps increase lift during takeoff and landing.

Tail fin

Spoilers act as brakes to create drag. This slows the plane down.

Jet engine

The rudder works with the ailerons to turn the plane left or right.

INVENTOR

Inventor: Sir Frank Whittle
Invention: Turbo jet engine
Date: 1930
The story: British pilot Sir Frank Whittle designed the first turbo jet engine when he was in the Royal Air Force. After his first ideas were rejected, he kept redesigning until he had a workable model.

Speedboats

As their name implies, speedboats are designed to go fast. Their hulls are made from light materials, such as fiberglass, aluminum, or plywood. Speedboats also have a streamlined shape. A motor drives a propeller that pushes a jet of water out the back, giving the boats their thrust.

Outboard Motor

An outboard motor is attached to the back of the hull with a clamp. It works in a similar way to a car engine. By opening up the throttle, the outboard motor burns more fuel. This makes the propeller turn faster, increasing the speed.

Propeller

Water jet

The propeller has angled blades to reduce turbulence in the water.

INVENTOR

Inventor: Josef Ressel

Invention: Screw propeller

Date: 1826

The story: Czech-Austrian inventor Josef Ressel came up with the idea to place a screw propeller onto the steam engine of a ship rather than a paddle wheel. His propeller gave ships more power and speed.

Inboard Motor

The hull encloses an inboard motor, which is connected to a driveshaft that spins the propeller. The engine is cooled by water pumped in from outside of the boat. Then, the water is ejected out the back with the exhaust.

Water jet

Propeller

Water intake

The hull of a speedboat is designed to skim the surface of the water at high speeds.

Rudder

The rudder is the main device used to steer a boat. It can be connected to the back of the boat or to the outboard motor. When the rudder turns, it deflects water and changes the direction of the boat.

Rudder

Hovercraft

A hovercraft levitates, or hovers, on a cushion of air. This allows it to travel over uneven surfaces, such as swampy grounds, stormy waters, and icy landscapes. A hovercraft can even glide smoothly from the sea straight up onto a beach.

Airflow

A hovercraft is a simple machine. It has a large downward-pointing fan that is powered by a diesel or gasoline engine. This fan creates the lift that raises the hovercraft above the surface. A rubber skirt traps a cushion of air under the craft.

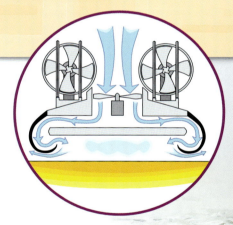

Changing Direction

The engine also powers other fans that propel the craft forward, backward, or sideways. Rudders positioned behind each fan change the direction of where the air flows, enabling the hovercraft to turn.

Skirts can be simple rubber bags or more complex designs with hundreds of fingers to maintain an even airflow.

INVENTOR

Inventor: Sir Christopher Cockerell

Invention: Hovercraft

Date: 1956

The story: British engineer Sir Christopher Cockerell got the idea for the hovercraft while building cabin cruisers for boat and van rental companies. He placed a can of cat food inside a larger coffee tin and used a vacuum cleaner to reverse the airflow, proving that his concept worked.

Ice has less friction than other surfaces, which means the hovercraft travels faster over it.

DID YOU KNOW? The average speed of a hovercraft is 35 mph (55 kph).

25

Submarines

Submarines are designed to travel below water as well as on its surface. When on the surface, a submarine uses a diesel engine to work its propeller. If the submarine is submerged, it is powered by a nuclear reactor or an electric motor.

Sonar

Light does not penetrate far underwater, so submarines navigate by sound navigation and ranging, or sonar. A sonar system emits pulses of sound waves through the water. These reflect off objects and their echoes return to the submarine, where they are picked up by sensitive microphones. A computer uses these signals to construct a detailed image of the space around the sub.

Ballast Tank

Submarines can stay submerged for months at a time. They sink and float by emptying and refilling their ballast tanks with air or water.

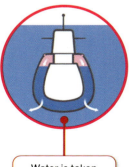

Water is taken in, and the submarine sinks.

Air is pumped in, forcing the water out, and the submarine rises.

When the ballast tanks are filled with air, the weight of the submarine becomes equal to the weight of the water it displaces. This causes the submarine to float on the surface.

Sometimes, a periscope is mounted on top of a raised tower called the conning tower. It lets the crew see above water while the vessel is submerged.

Modern submarines can dive deeper than earlier ones.

Inventor: Cornelis Drebbel

Invention: Submarine

Date: 1620

The story: Dutch engineer Cornelis Drebbel built the first submarine that could be steered. Its wooden frame was covered with leather. The submarine was powered by oars and the force of the current. It could remain submerged for about three hours.

INVENTOR

DID YOU KNOW? Submarines do not have windows. Instead, many use underwater cameras to see what is happening around them.

Drones

Drones are uncrewed aerial vehicles. They can take off and land vertically, hover, and fly in different directions. Quadcopter drones are popular because they are affordable and easy to control.

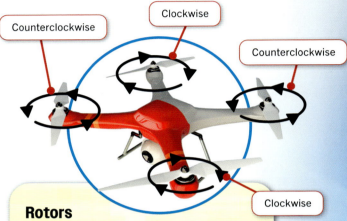

Counterclockwise

Clockwise

Counterclockwise

Clockwise

Quadcopter drones are flown using remote control units. The controllers can take the form of a game pad, smartphone, or tablet.

Rotors

The lift and thrust of a quadcopter drone is provided by four rotors that spin in different directions. They are mounted on spokes. As the rotors push down on the air, the air pushes up on the rotors. The faster the rotors spin, the greater the lift. To turn, one pair of rotors must spin more slowly than the other pair.

Sensors

Onboard sensors keep drones in the air. An altimeter tells the drone how far it is from the ground. GPS chips provide information on its position and direction of travel. They let users set a return destination if the drone loses radio contact. Drones can also have laser or heat sensors.

DID YOU KNOW? Drones can help save lives. They are used to send medical supplies to remote areas.

Rotor

The frame is made of lightweight materials, such as plastic. Inside are the electronics.

Rotor

Sensors

Drones are usually equipped with a compact, high-definition camera that has a wide-angle lens with a field of vision covering up to 180 degrees. This lens is known as a fisheye.

Inventor: Igor Sikorsky
Invention: Helicopter
Date: 1939
The story: Russian aircraft designer Igor Sikorsky invented the helicopter. His design had rotating blades—the same basis of drones.

INVENTOR

Passenger Drones

Most of the drones we see flying above our heads today are small and controlled from afar. They are used for photography, small package delivery, or surveillance. But drones do not have to be small—or even uncrewed!

In 2016, a Chinese company produced the world's first passenger drone. It could carry only one person at a time, but its four propellers could zip the drone along at more than 60 mph (97 kph). The company soon followed up with a two-passenger drone with fixed wings and eight dual-rotor wing blades.

Several companies are now developing four- and five-passenger drones. They hope the drones can be used as airport shuttles, taxis, or emergency response vehicles. Passenger drones may help reduce traffic on crowded roads. They could fly in a straight line from one place to another, without having to follow curving and congested roads. This could greatly reduce travel time.

DID YOU KNOW? In the late 1480s, inventor Leonardo da Vinci made sketches for a flying machine that looked very similar to a modern helicopter.

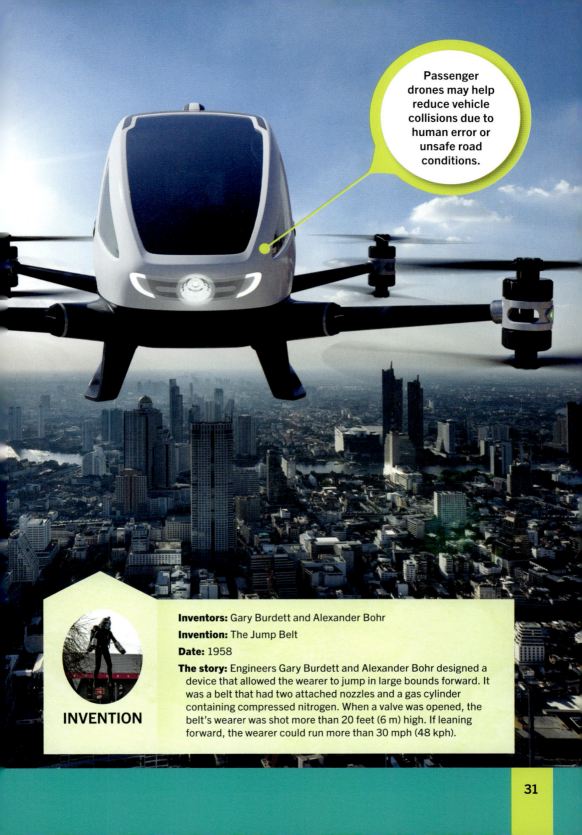

Passenger drones may help reduce vehicle collisions due to human error or unsafe road conditions.

INVENTION

Inventors: Gary Burdett and Alexander Bohr

Invention: The Jump Belt

Date: 1958

The story: Engineers Gary Burdett and Alexander Bohr designed a device that allowed the wearer to jump in large bounds forward. It was a belt that had two attached nozzles and a gas cylinder containing compressed nitrogen. When a valve was opened, the belt's wearer was shot more than 20 feet (6 m) high. If leaning forward, the wearer could run more than 30 mph (48 kph).

Spacecraft

Today, thousands of spacecraft are circling Earth, sending us data and relaying telecommunication signals. Robotic probes are being sent on missions to explore the planets, moons, comets, and asteroids of our solar system. The biggest spacecraft ever built—the International Space Station (ISS)—is currently in orbit around Earth.

ISS Structure

The ISS is made up of pressurized modules containing living quarters and laboratories for the astronauts, as well as solar arrays for power. It has six robotic arms that are used to carry out remote-controlled repairs and connect arriving spacecraft.

Docking ports enable other spacecraft to connect to the space station.

DID YOU KNOW? The first space shuttle, *Columbia*, was launched in 1981. It was in service for 22 years and completed 27 missions.

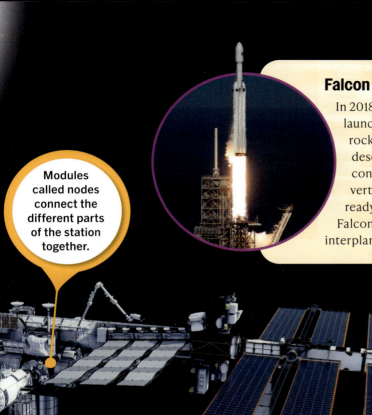

Falcon Heavy

In 2018, SpaceX successfully launched the Falcon Heavy rocket. The rocket descended to Earth in a controlled drop and landed vertically on the launch pad, ready to be reused. The Falcon Heavy is suitable for interplanetary missions.

Modules called nodes connect the different parts of the station together.

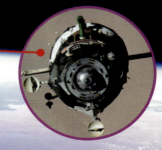

The Russian Soyuz spacecraft have taken people and supplies to and from the ISS.

INVENTOR

Inventor: Dr. Robert H. Goddard

Invention: First rocket to use liquid fuel

Date: 1926

The story: American physicist Dr. Robert H. Goddard invented the first rocket to use liquid fuel. Before this, all rockets had been propelled by burning solid fuel. Dr. Robert H. Goddard's rocket flew 184 ft. (56 m) at 60 mph (100 kph).

Planetary Rovers

Much of the information we have about the surface of our moon and Mars, our nearest planetary neighbor, has not been gathered from crewed space flights. Instead, reliable and durable rovers have done most of the hard work of exploration. They have collected soil samples, photographed and mapped surfaces, and sought evidence of water or past life.

Rovers are solar-powered wheeled vehicles that are dropped off on a planetary surface by a spacecraft. While some are designed to carry human space crews, most are uncrewed. Rovers are made to withstand temperature extremes, space dust, and cosmic rays, with the hope that they can keep working for several years.

Because radio signals take a long time to reach distant bodies, such as the moon and Mars, rovers are not remote-controlled. A command issued from Earth would take as long as 21 minutes to reach a rover on Mars. Instead, rovers are programmed to direct themselves with very little input from human controllers as they navigate the surface and collect samples and data.

DID YOU KNOW? Engineers are working on designs for rovers without wheels. Rovers may someday be walking, running, or leaping on the surfaces of distant planets.

Cameras detect obstacles in a rover's path.

Wheels help a rover move across the terrain.

INVENTOR

Inventor: Wernher von Braun

Invention: Lunar rover

Date: 1952

The story: Seventeen years before the first astronauts landed on the moon, German-American aerospace engineer Wernher von Braun introduced the idea of a pressurized rover. It could carry astronauts across the lunar surface during exploratory expeditions. He also created detailed plans for a rotating, wheel-shaped space station.

Weather Satellites

Weather satellites circle the skies, carrying sensors to detect visible, infrared, and microwave radiation. These instruments scan Earth to create digitized images that are transmitted to receiving stations on the ground. Meteorologists then study and interpret the images sent from these satellites. There are two types of weather satellites.

Geostationary Satellites

Geostationary satellites hover over the same spot at Earth's equator by orbiting the planet at the same speed that Earth turns. From an altitude of about 23,000 miles (35,000 km), they scan the same geographical area continuously.

Weather satellite data is transmitted to receiving stations. Then, it gets relayed to weather forecast organizations all over the world.

Polar Satellites

Polar satellites orbit Earth at an altitude of about 500 miles (800 km). They move north and south, passing over both poles in a single orbit. Two polar satellites can monitor a location once every six hours.

Data from weather satellites helps meteorologists make short- and long-term weather forecasts.

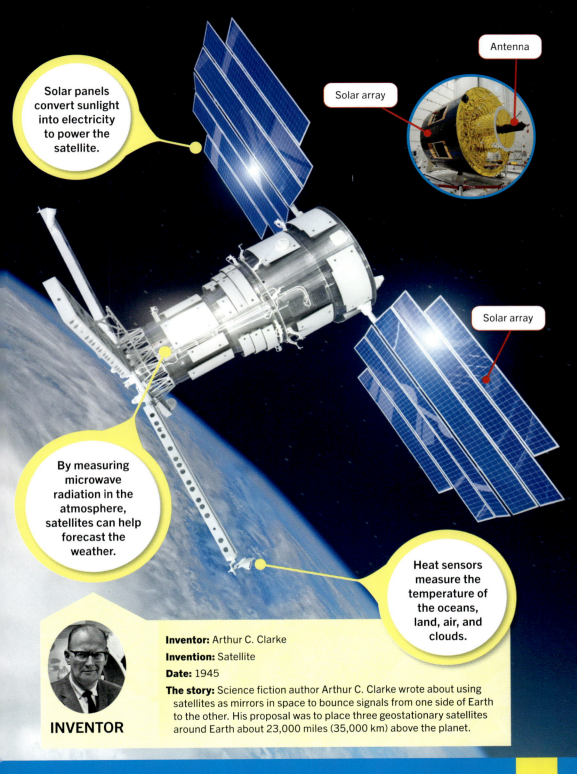

Solar panels convert sunlight into electricity to power the satellite.

Antenna

Solar array

Solar array

By measuring **microwave radiation** in the atmosphere, satellites can help forecast the weather.

Heat sensors measure the temperature of the oceans, land, air, and clouds.

Inventor: Arthur C. Clarke

Invention: Satellite

Date: 1945

The story: Science fiction author Arthur C. Clarke wrote about using satellites as mirrors in space to bounce signals from one side of Earth to the other. His proposal was to place three geostationary satellites around Earth about 23,000 miles (35,000 km) above the planet.

INVENTOR

DID YOU KNOW? The first satellite launched was the Russian spacecraft *Sputnik 1* in 1957.

37

GPS

GPS stands for Global Positioning System, a worldwide navigation system based in space. It consists of 30 satellites located in 6 orbits around Earth, with 4 operational satellites and a spare satellite in each orbit. A GPS receiver on Earth, often called a satnav, works in conjunction with the satellites to calculate a precise location.

Navigation Satellites

There are at least four GPS satellites that are able to transmit to any point on Earth at all times. Each satellite constantly transmits information about its position and the exact time. These signals travel at the speed of light.

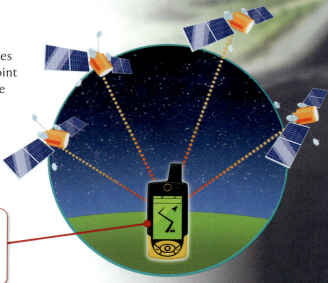

A satnav locates four or more satellites, calculates its distance from each, and uses this information to calculate its own location.

INVENTOR

Inventor: Gladys West

Invention: Global positioning calculations

Date: 1950s and 1960s

The story: American mathematician Gladys West worked at a U.S. Navy base in Virginia, where she recorded satellite locations and calculated the size and shape of Earth. Her work contributed to the accuracy of GPS.

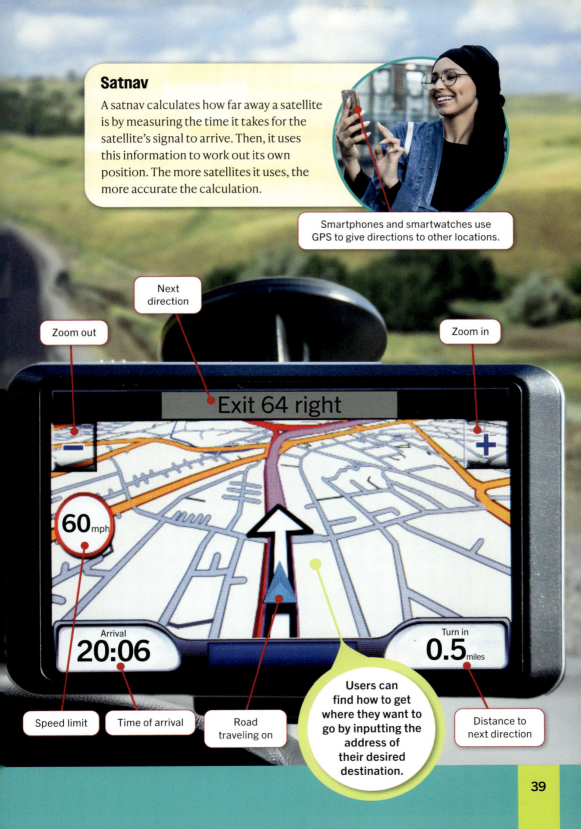

Satnav

A satnav calculates how far away a satellite is by measuring the time it takes for the satellite's signal to arrive. Then, it uses this information to work out its own position. The more satellites it uses, the more accurate the calculation.

Smartphones and smartwatches use GPS to give directions to other locations.

Next direction

Zoom out

Zoom in

Exit 64 right

60mph

Arrival
20:06

Turn in
0.5miles

Speed limit

Time of arrival

Road traveling on

Users can find how to get where they want to go by inputting the address of their desired destination.

Distance to next direction

Cranes

There are two main types of cranes: tower cranes and mobile cranes. Tower cranes are fixed to the ground and are used to build tall buildings. They are built using a mobile crane, which is located on the back of a truck. First, the mobile crane builds the foundation of the tower crane and then adds the tower or mast. The cab and jib are then placed into position. Once a pulley system is in place, the tower crane uses its own hook to build itself up further. It adds one section at a time inside a climbing frame.

A large concrete counterweight balances the load on the jib, stopping the crane from toppling over.

Climbing frame

New section

This shows how a tower crane builds itself taller.

INVENTOR

Inventor: Hans Liebherr

Invention: Mobile crane

Date: 1949

The story: German master builder Hans Liebherr designed and built the first revolving mobile crane. It moved from site to site on the back of a truck, using hydraulics to lift things.

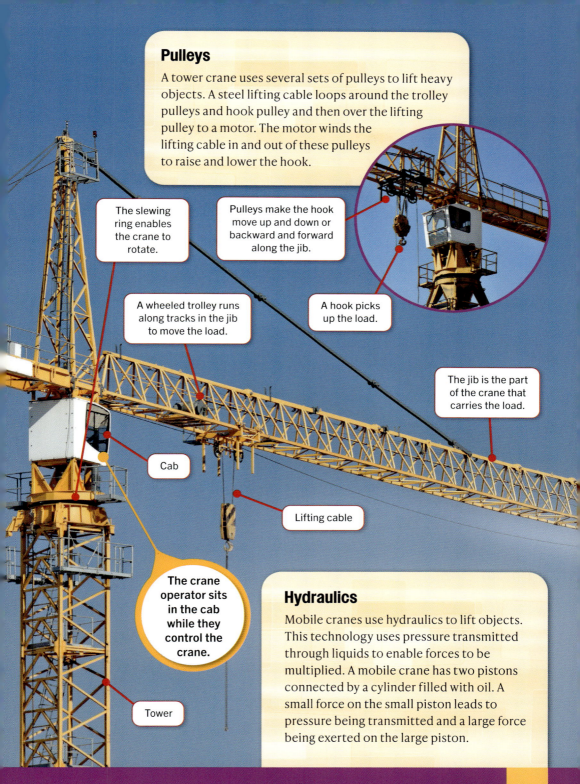

Pulleys

A tower crane uses several sets of pulleys to lift heavy objects. A steel lifting cable loops around the trolley pulleys and hook pulley and then over the lifting pulley to a motor. The motor winds the lifting cable in and out of these pulleys to raise and lower the hook.

The slewing ring enables the crane to rotate.

Pulleys make the hook move up and down or backward and forward along the jib.

A wheeled trolley runs along tracks in the jib to move the load.

A hook picks up the load.

The jib is the part of the crane that carries the load.

Cab

Lifting cable

The crane operator sits in the cab while they control the crane.

Tower

Hydraulics

Mobile cranes use hydraulics to lift objects. This technology uses pressure transmitted through liquids to enable forces to be multiplied. A mobile crane has two pistons connected by a cylinder filled with oil. A small force on the small piston leads to pressure being transmitted and a large force being exerted on the large piston.

DID YOU KNOW? The earliest cranes were built by the ancient Greeks.

41

Transportation for the Future

Technology is always changing. Within just 150 years, humans went from walking on foot and riding horses to moving on bikes, trains, cars, and even rocket ships.

Before the end of the 21st century, we can expect many more changes. Designers and engineers are working to create self-driving cars and buses, flying cars, passenger drones, and electric jumbo jets. In the future, there may even be passenger pods that travel through tunnels at more than 500 mph (805 kph)!

We may be traveling through space and time in ways we cannot even imagine yet. What kinds of new vehicles can you dream up? With a lot of studying, hard work, and trial and error, maybe you will make that dream a reality!

Most flying cars are being designed to carry up to two passengers.

Flying cars may reduce air pollution, helping the environment while getting us where we need to go.

Review and Reflect

Now that you've read about technology used in vehicles and transportation, let's review what you've learned. Use the following questions to reflect on your newfound knowledge and integrate it with what you already knew.

Check for Understanding

1. Name two parts of a bicycle and describe what each does. *(See pp. 6–7)*

2. Explain how e-bike motors work. *(See pp. 8–9)*

3. Which car safety features help protect drivers and passengers? Which ones help prevent accidents? *(See pp. 14–15)*

4. What controls traffic lights? *(See pp. 16–17)*

5. How do train wheels and tracks work? *(See pp. 18–19)*

6. Name at least three parts of a plane and explain what each does. *(See pp. 20–21)*

7. What's the difference between an outboard motor and an inboard motor? *(See pp. 22–23)*

8. What holds a hovercraft off the ground? *(See pp. 24–25)*

9. How does sonar work? *(See pp. 26–27)*

10. List three parts of a drone and explain what each one does. *(See pp. 28–29)*

11. What can drones be used for? *(See pp. 30–31)*

12. What are rovers? How do they send information? *(See pp. 34–35)*

13. Explain the differences between a geostationary satellite and a polar satellite. *(See pp. 36–37)*

14. How do satellites work with GPS? *(See pp. 38–39)*

15. What are the two types of cranes? How do they work? *(See pp. 40–41)*

Making Connections

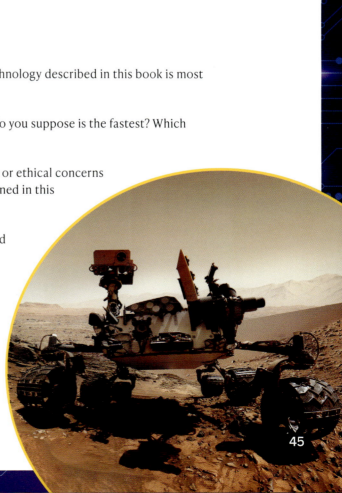

1. Compare and contrast the ways gas cars, hybrid cars, and electric cars get power.

2. Find at least three safety features listed in the book. Which do you think is most valuable?

3. Choose two inventors mentioned in the book. In your own words, how did what they made affect society? What do their inventions have in common?

4. Explain how one of the inventions from this book evolved over time.

5. Several of the vehicles in this book use engines. Choose two of these to compare and contrast. How do they work? Where does their energy come from?

In Your Own Words

1. Which type of transportation or technology described in this book is most interesting to you? Why?

2. Which type of vehicle in this book do you suppose is the fastest? Which one uses the most energy?

3. Do you see any potential drawbacks or ethical concerns about any of the technology mentioned in this book? What might they be?

4. How do you think transportation and vehicles will change in the future?

5. Why do people continue to design new kinds of transportation?

Glossary

aileron a hinged surface in the trailing edge of an aircraft wing, used to control the roll of an aircraft

antenna a rod, dish, or other structure by which radio signals are transmitted or received

exhaust waste gases expelled from an engine or other machine

friction the resistance that one surface or object encounters when moving over another

induction the production of an electric current through being near an electrified or magnetized body

infrared having a wavelength greater than that of the red end of the visible light spectrum but less than that of microwaves

laser a device that generates an intense beam of light through the emission of photons from excited atoms or molecules

magnetic field a region around a magnet within which the force of magnetism acts

piston a disk within an internal-combustion engine or pump that fits within a cylinder and moves up and down against a liquid or gas

pulley a wheel with a grooved rim around which a cord passes; a pulley is used to change the direction of a force applied to the cord to raise heavy weights

radiation the emission of energy in the form of electromagnetic waves

rudder a flat piece hinged vertically near the stern of a boat that is used for steering

sensor a device that detects, measures, or records external activity

spoiler a flap on the wing of an aircraft that can be deployed to create drag and reduce speed

telecommunication communication over a distance by, for example, wire or radio signals

turbine a rotor that is turned by the flow of wind, water, steam, or some other fluid in order to generate power

vacuum a space from which the air has been removed

valve a device for controlling the passage of fluid through a pipe or duct

wavelength the distance between successive crests of an electromagnetic wave

Read More

Colson, Rob. *Supercars (Motormania)*. New York: Crabtree Publishing, 2022.

Heitkamp, Kristina Lyn. *Electric Vehicles (Focus on Current Events)*. Lake Elmo, MN: Focus Readers, 2022.

Kim, Carol. *Hidden Heroes in Technology (Who Else in History?)*. Minneapolis: Lerner Publications, 2023.

Kirkfield, Vivian. *From Here to There: Inventions That Changed the Way the World Moves*. Boston: Houghton Mifflin Harcourt, 2021.

Learn More Online

1. Go to **www.factsurfer.com** or scan the QR code below.
2. Enter "**Vehicles Transport Tech**" into the search box.
3. Click on the cover of this book to see a list of websites.

Index